How To
EAT A ROSE

Published by
Long Creek Herbs
P.O. Box 127
Blue Eye, MO 65611
417-779-5450
Lcherbs@interlinc.net
www.Longcreekherbs.com

ISBN 1-889791-16-4

Introduction

*"**Herb**: Any of various often aromatic plants used especially in medicine or as seasoning."* **American Heritage Dictionary, Second College Edition.**

No one knows who the first person was to eat a rose, but if you walk in the still virgin prairies of the Midwest where I grew up, in early spring, when the dew is just beginning to dry and the butterflies are starting their work, when you bend down and stick your nose into a sweet, pink, wild rose, you can't help but notice the power of the flower on all of your senses. The fragrance bombards your nose, your taste buds, and even your memory, in ways that few other flowers can. It's not difficult to imagine some curious person in prehistory, deciding if the rose smelled that good, then it must taste good, too, and taking a bite. From such an experiment was perhaps born the first attempts with ways to eat the rose.

Roses are the most recognized flower in our culture. We celebrate birthdays and anniversaries with them, we use them as a symbol of love, of innocence and purity, in all sorts of cultural events throughout our daily lives.

In our own country, a frenzy of commercial rose buying takes place each Valentine's Day with exorbitant prices and people vying for the best or the most or the last, roses on the florist's shelves. No other flower commands such power in our culture.

In areas of the world where civilizations have thrived for millennia, roses are used for flavoring much like we in the West use vanilla or cinnamon. Rose ice cream is a common flavor in Asian countries. Rose drinks are a regular cooling summer drink in desert areas and rose water splashed on the forehead to cool the face is as common in some cultures as a cologne or after shave lotion is to ours.

Early Romans used rose water in their official government fountains and rose water was also used to wash the walls and floors to purify temples.

In the desert regions of Afghanistan, delightfully fragrant rose water is added to fresh, cool water as it is drawn from a spring, for a refreshing cool drink that is offered to visitors.

In India, where the rose is considered the king of all flowers, it is used in both religious and secular celebrations. You will find roses strung into garlands for festivals, used lavishly in weddings and in temples, and incorporated into the foods and beverages for those events.

When I visited New Delhi on Republic Day, India's equivalent of our Fourth of July, I saw government helicopters flying over the crowds of celebrants, dropping tons of fresh, fragrant rose petals over the people.

Rose petals used in this manner have a soothing, peaceful effect and is one of the simplest forms of aromatherapy. In that country, also, you will find roses being used as the flavoring in gulab jamun (translated from Hindi, it means, "rose fruit") a delicate dessert the size and shape of donut holes, floating in rose water and honey.

In remote regions of Turkey, a rose water sprinkler can still be found on most every dinner table, not unlike the catsup bottle is on ours. The rose water sprinkler is common in India, as well, where it is called an attardarne.

Here in America we tend to look upon the rose as just a flower in a vase. Roses are used for lotions and rinses for the body, too, but it is their uses in foods that is fascinating to me. Rose ice cream, sharbet (a sweet beverage), rose wine, rose vinegar, rose candies, jams and jellies, are all an important part of life in many cultures.

I treat the rose as an herb, more than a flower because of the many uses it has beyond just looking pretty in a vase. Rosemary is pretty in a vase, too, yet it is always thought of as an herb. The rose has a much broader history of use in medicines, crafts and cooking than rosemary ever did! Therefore, as far as I am concerned, the rose is an herb in my garden.

I first began using roses in salads when I was a teenager. I had watched an old black and white movie, the name of which escapes me, in which the star ate a gardenia. I remember it sparked in me a curiosity about eating flowers that has never left me.

Soon I had munched my way through my mother's flower garden (researching first what was edible and what should be avoided).

That same summer, all of the boys and girls in our local 4-H club decided to take a Foods Project together. On a weekly basis we met at our project leader's house and practiced making simple dishes.

I began bringing salads to our group, liberally strewn with flowers of some sort. Mostly I used roses, sprinkling the petals over the tops of my creations. I used wild prairie roses and the intensely fragrant rugosa roses from my mother's garden. Sometimes I used other flowers, such as strawberry and garden pea blossoms, lilacs, and pansies. But roses were the primary flower I liked. In the 1950s, it was a pretty bizarre thing to do, especially for a 4-H Club Beginning Cooking class, but it was the girls who made faces and complained at the idea of eating a flower. The boys took it as a challenge to eat weird things. Everyone was equally surprised that roses actually tasted good, and soon my strange flower dishes became standard fare.

I found that my mother's rose bushes which grew the largest, and had the most thorns, also had the most flavorful flowers. One waist-high bush held incredibly fragrant clusters of half dollar sized, dainty, white, double flowers which rebloomed throughout the summer. That particular rose, I later learned, dates back several hundred years. Those were good on the tops of desserts (even though my father and grandfather always looked at that topping with suspicion and scraped them off). My mother, showing her support, always tasted my unusual concoctions.

An old, shoulder high, rugosa shrub rose that grew near my parents' bedroom window, had the most heavenly fragrance and the best flavor for culinary purposes. It bloomed heavily in June, then again, sporadically, throughout the summer. The flowers were about five inches across, double, a deep rose color, and so fragrant you could almost float on the aroma. I turned some of those into rose vinegar and cooked some into rose syrups.

In those early years I began collecting ways to use roses. I adapted recipes from various sources, experimented, and found new ways to use the flavor of this remarkable plant.

Throughout these pages I have assembled recipes for all kinds of ways to eat and use the rose. Some are my own, some are adapted from ancient recipes and some are contributed by friends. I hope you enjoy all these ways to eat a rose.

What Kind of Roses Should Be Used for Food?

Roses, to be used as food, should be pesticide free, organically grown (or at least grown without the pesticide, fungicide and fertilizer mix that is often placed in the soil around a rose bush and taken up through the roots and stems).

Roses for food should be only fragrant, old-fashioned (or "antique") roses. Florist's roses won't work. Why?

1 - Florist roses are almost without fragrance. It's the variety of rose they use, grown for gorgeous flowers without thought to fragrance.

2 - Florist roses are highly sprayed with pesticides during their growing cycle. (Many are grown in third world countries where there are no restrictions on the use of chemicals such as DDT and other banned pesticides in the U.S.) Since they aren't thought of as food here, there is little regulation of what is sprayed on the rose during its growth.

3 - Florist roses have no flavor. It's been bred out of them, not intentionally, but as a result of the "bigger is better" concept for long-stemmed, perfect roses.

For the best roses for food, choose very fragrant roses, from bushes that have been grown without chemicals. After all, if you eat the rose, you don't want, also, to ingest pesticides!

Pick roses in early morning when the dew has just left but before the heat of the day. The fragrance and flavor will be at their highest then.

Old-fashioned shrub or antique roses work best for flavoring and food, roses such as *Rosa rugosa* and others. These have the added advantage of not requiring pesticides or fungicides to grow and produce roses (unlike tea roses which won't survive in most climates unless they are constantly sprayed and pampered). Tea roses also have little fragrance compared to the antique rose varieties.

"An herb is any plant that is beneficial to man," Steven Foster, *author of the* **Peterson Field Guide to Medicinal Plants.**

HONEYS, JELLIES, SYRUPS AND JAMS

Rose Honey

I have adapted the instructions for making Rose Honey from an old English recipe, which is more like a syrup than honey:

- 1 cup dried red rose petals
- 2 cups water
- 4 cups honey

Bring the water to a boil and pour over the rose petals. Stir and let steep for 24 hours. Strain, discarding the flowers and add the honey. Bring the liquid to a boil and simmer until reduced by one third. Add a few drops of red food coloring if desired.

Use rose honey for cooking: add to cake frosting instead of vanilla; drizzle some over ice cream; use for a topping for pound cake; use 1/4 cup of the honey to sweeten fresh fruit instead of sugar. This syrup is also soothing for sore throats.

Real Rose Honey

Here's a really tasty rose honey that I like to serve on freshly baked lemon balm muffins.

- 2 cups light-colored honey
- 2 cups freshly picked very fragrant rose petals

Warm honey in the microwave until hot. Combine the rose petals and honey and stir well, cover with plastic wrap and leave unrefrigerated for 24 hours. Warm the honey in the microwave again so that the honey is fully liquid and strain out the rose petals. The honey is now ready to refrigerate. Let stand at room temperature for about an hour before serving.

Instant Rose Honey

This one is so simple you'll laugh. You can whip this up after guests arrive and while muffins are baking. Or, serve this with fresh buttermilk biscuits at breakfast and your guests will feel they've been treated very special.

- 3 cups fragrant rose petals
- 3/4 cup honey

Put the fresh rose petals in the food processor and pulse process until you have well shredded petals. Pour them out into a dish and add the honey, mixing well. Serve immediately and refrigerate any leftovers for up to 5 days.

Colonial Rose Preserves

This was called "rose tobacco" in Colonial times. It's a simple recipe and is delicious used like jam on muffins or toast.

- 1 cup rose petals
- 1 cup brown sugar

Alternate layers of petals and sugar in a plastic zip bag. Before zipping the bag closed, push out all of the air inside, then zip it closed and make sure it is sealed well. Once every day for 3 days, massage the bag a bit to move around the materials inside, then set it aside in the refrigerator. In about a month the rose flavor will be well mixed with the sugar and it will be all one mixture of sweet, rosy preserves.

Rose Petal Jelly

Rose petal jelly is perfect for small tea cakes and tea sandwiches. It combines well with cream cheese, with rose petals, mint leaves, slices of freshly baked sponge cake; it's even wonderfully elegant spread on angel food cake and made into little dessert sandwiches.

- 1 1/2 cup fragrant pink or red rose petals
- 1 1/2 cup bottled or frozen white grape juice
- 1/2 cup bottled water
- 3 1/2 c sugar
- 1 package liquid fruit pectin

Taste the white part of one of the rose petals. If it is bitter (some are, some aren't), cut off the small, white part of the rose petals. Bring the white grape juice and water to a rolling boil and add the rose petals. Stir and cook one minute. Add fruit pectin; cook stirring constantly, until mixture returns to a rolling boil. Continue boiling one minute, stirring frequently.

Remove from heat and skim off foam with a metal spoon, but leave most of the rose petals in the jelly. (Add one or two drops of red food color at this point if you want the jelly to have more color). Quickly pour jelly into hot sterilized jars leaving 1/4 in head space in each jar; cover with metal lids and screw tight. Process in boiling water bath for five minutes. Makes 3 pints.

Rose Syrup

For a stunningly good dessert, serve this syrup over a plain slice of sponge cake, add several fresh rose petals and three or four fresh red raspberries. Ahh! It is such an elegant dessert and so easy.

- 1 cup fragrant pink or red rose petals, white parts removed (if bitter)
- 1 cup filtered, spring or bottled water
- 1 1/2 cups sugar
- 3 whole cloves

Combine rose petals and water in a sauce pan and bring to boil. Simmer for five minutes. Add the sugar and cloves. Simmer only until sugar dissolves; strain out and discard the petals. Store in a jar in the refrigerator or freezer. Makes 1 2/3 cup.

Rose Hip Sauce

- 2 cups fresh rose hips, stem and top removed, hips cut open and seeds removed
- 4 cups water
- 2 1/2 cups sugar
- 2 tablespoons freshly chopped lemon balm
- 2 teaspoons fresh lemon juice

Chop rose hips in food processor. Bring water to a boil and add rose hips, simmering 5 minutes. Add the lemon balm and lemon juice and continue cooking for another 5 minutes. Remove from heat, cover pan and let steep for an hour. Strain, bring liquid to a boil and add sugar. Simmer for 5 minutes (or more if you want the syrup to be thicker). Cool and refrigerate until ready to use, or freeze in plastic container. To use: Add a tablespoon of the syrup to a cup of freshly boiled water, stir and drink for a pleasant winter beverage.

Gulukand - Rose Paste, or Jam

Gulukand, in India, is used as a flavoring in sweet dishes and is also eaten like jam. It has a pleasant flavor and medicinally is considered good for reducing boils, keeping skin and blood circulation clean. It is also used in sweetening betel leaf, which is a popular mouth freshener, served in restaurants after a meal.

Remove the fresh rose petals from one very fragrant red or pink rose and spread them in a ten ounce plastic or glass container (remember to cut off the white parts if they are bitter). Sprinkle a teaspoon of sugar over the petals. Repeat this layering, of rose petals and sugar until you have filled a ten ounce container. Cover the container for ten to fifteen days. The sugar will draw out the flavor and fragrance from the petals and form a syrup. At this point, put the petals and the syrup into a food processor and pulse blend, making a paste (the traditional way was to use a mortar and pestle). Then put the rose paste into a small container with a lid and keep in the refrigerator. The gulukand, or rose paste, is ready to use, like a jam or jelly, as well as a flavoring in cakes, cookies and other desserts.

SANDWICHES

Rose Sandwiches

When I was a child in the 1950s it was a popular thing in our community for young married farm wives to get together for a social afternoon. They'd trade child raising stories, let the young children play, and give the mothers a chance to visit. This was back when the State Extension offices were filled with energetic and creative sorts who sent out recipes to young families. And, too, Ladies' Home Journal *and* Better Homes and Gardens *were filled with ideas for "party foods."*

Each month a different housewife was host to these parties, and she would have already read the latest recipes for "the perfect party." Each lady would try to out-do the previous month's host. I was 4 or 5 when I first encountered mint leaves in iced tea, and that time also dates my first memories of little finger sandwiches with the crusts cut off. (And I remember thinking how thoughtful the host was for making sandwiches just the size for a my little hands).

One of these sandwiches was a big hit and all the women felt a bit racy and adventurous by sampling this sandwich, since it was made of something not usually thought of as in our community edible. Rose sandwiches were a hit, and here are three ways for making them.

Virginia's Rose Sandwiches

Several thin slices of homemade white bread (you can use frozen bread dough, baked according to directions; make the bread a day ahead, then wrap it as it will slice easier the second day).

- About 2 cups of loose fragrant rose petals, red and pink both if available
- 4 tablespoons unsalted butter, room temperature

Virginia's Rose Sandwiches, continued...

Spread a slice of bread with butter, spreading it edge to edge. Place a layer of rose petals on the butter, then butter another slice of bread and repeat by layering rose petals across that one. Place the two slices together, rose petals to rose petals. Fix 3 or 4 of these large sandwiches, then place on a cutting board and with cookie cutter, cut out the sandwiches. Or, with a sharp knife, cut the sandwiches into finger sized pieces with the crusts removed. Chill briefly and serve on a crystal plate covered with rose leaves.

Mom's Rose Sandwiches

- Angel food cake, preferably 2 days old, so as to slice easier
- 1- 4 oz. package cream cheese, room temperature
- 2 cups fragrant rose petals, any color

Slice the angel food cake (homemade or commercial) into slices about 1/2 inch thick. Carefully spread each slice on one side with a layer of cream cheese, then place a layer of rose petals, as if you were putting lettuce on a sandwich. Repeat with the other slice with cream cheese and rose petals. Put the sandwich pieces together, then cut into finger sized pieces, such as diamonds, rounds, etc. Top each sandwich with a candied rose petal and a candied mint leaf. Serve with iced rose tea. Children love these for tea parties, too!

Rose Sandwiches

- 4 slices whole grain or European style bread
- 2 leaves Romaine lettuce
- The petals from 2 large flowered fragrant roses
- 1/4 cup goat cheese
- 2 tablespoons walnuts
- Sweet, fresh red onion rings
- *Raspberry yogurt dressing
- Butter, at room temperature

Spread butter thinly over one side of all 4 slices of bread. Spread the rose petals over two slices of the bread, add the lettuce leaf, then half the goat cheese and walnuts, divided between the two slices. Add the onion rings and drizzle the raspberry yogurt dressing over the cheese and walnuts, or simply spread a generous layer on the remaining two slices of bread, combine, slice the sandwiches in halves or triangles and serve. (For a less hearty, more decorative sandwich, leave off the top slice of bread and serve open faced).

*Raspberry-Rose Yogurt Dressing
- 1/2 cup raspberry yogurt
- 1/2 teaspoon food grade rose water

Stir together well and serve over mixed salad greens like the traditional bitter/mild European mixes.

Tea Sandwiches

Roses are elegant used in sandwiches instead of lettuce. Here's one variation of the tea sandwich which will delight your tea time guests. Remember, these sandwiches are dainty little morsels of food for eating while sipping tea over pleasant conversation. Don't expect to feed a lumberjack with these!

- 1/2 cup rose petals
- Sponge cake, sliced about 1/2 inch thick or less
- Whipped cream cheese, at room temperature
- Pinch of ground cinnamon mixed with a teaspoon of powdered sugar

Lay out the slices of sponge cake and spread each with a moderate layer of whipped cream cheese. Give a faint, tiny dusting of cinnamon sugar; don't overdue it, less is best!

On top of one slice of the cake, spread a generous layer of the fresh rose petals. Add the other piece of cake for the top. Repeat until you have "sandwiches." Now, cut the sandwiches into finger sandwiches, about two fingers wide and as long as the cake slices, so that you have lots of tiny sandwiches. Serve stacked on a platter on which you have scattered lots of very fragrant rose petals, with a few mint leaves for garnish.

Cucumber Sandwiches

For this you need some good white bread, or good quality Italian bread would work fine.

- 1 loaf of good quality white bread
- 1 cucumber, sliced and seeded
- 1-2 cups fresh, fragrant rose petals
- Butter, at room temperature
- Leaf lettuce
- Juice of 1/2 fresh lemon

Cucumber Sandwiches, continued...

Lay out the slices of bread and cut off the bread crusts. Spread each slice of bread on one side, with some butter that has been softened to room temperature. Don't use margarine! Use the real thing for this.

Slice the cucumber into a bowl and pour the lemon juice over it. Dust with salt if desired and leave in the juice for two or three minutes. Drain and pat dry.

Put a leaf of lettuce on the buttered bread. Add a layer of rose petals, then the cucumber slices and top with the other piece of buttered bread.

Cut the sandwiches into triangles. Cover until serving time. Can be refrigerated for a few hours then brought back to room temperature 20 minutes before serving.

SALADS, SALAD DRESSINGS, VINEGARS, SOUPS

Rose Raspberry Salad

This is an elegant yet simple salad to serve before a main course of salmon or other seafood. Use a balsamic vinegar (no oil, it's too heavy) for the dressing. (For this, choose a good quality blue cheese, such as Roquefort, Stilton or Gorgonzola).

- European or early spring lettuces, about 6 - 8 cups
- 1 cup fresh or frozen red raspberries
- 1/2 cup fresh red or pink, fragrant rose petals
- 1/2 cup blue cheese crumbles
- 1 tablespoon toasted sunflower seeds or toasted almonds

Arrange a helping of salad lettuce greens on each plate. Sprinkle fresh rose petals, several red raspberries and a generous helping of cheese crumbles over each. Top with the almond slices or sunflower seeds and drizzle a bit of balsamic vinegar over each salad. Just a little of the vinegar is sufficient. Don't toss the salad and serve it immediately.

Rose Vinegar #1

I made this on the Home Matters show, for the Discovery television channel a few years back. Both Susan Powell and Lee Meriweather, two former Miss Americas, liked this best of all the vinegars I made. The recipe is simple and the vinegar has many uses. Use it as a gargle for sore throat. Use the vinegar without oil for an excellent salad dressing. Sprinkle it on baked fish. Or, my favorite use: ***Roses in a Glass*** (a hot afternoon drink that should be sipped from a rocking chair on the garden porch)

One shot glass of rose vinegar in a glass of ice. Fill the glass with club soda , add a lemon twist and mint sprig and serve.

Rose Salad Vinegar

Gather enough rose petals to fill a quart jar. Be sure all the stems and hips are removed. Completely cover petals with cider vinegar (or use white wine vinegar or champagne vinegar). Cover with plastic wrap and set on kitchen counter. Shake vinegar once daily for 4 days. Strain out petals and discard. To this liquid, add a scant tablespoon of brown sugar and stir to dissolve.

Store in a dark place, such as pantry on in a kitchen cabinet. The vinegar will keep for up to a year.

Rose Salad Vinegar #2

Follow the directions above for Rose Vinegar: fill the jar with rose petals, add the vinegar, put away for ten days (omitting the 4 day, shaking part, above).

Strain out and discard the rose petals and fill the jar again with fresh roses. Pour back the original vinegar over the petals and let set another ten days.

At the end of the ten days, strain out and discard the petals. Put the vinegar in a pan and heat, not to boiling, but quite warm. Add 1 tablespoon of brown sugar and stir until dissolved.

Rose & Fruit Salad

Combine 4 cups of a combination of any of the following:
Seedless grapes, cantaloupe, honeydew, fresh or frozen peach slices, pears, pineapple spears, mango slices, watermelon balls, fresh plum slices, nectarine or kiwi slices or raspberries, and mix with this Marinade:
• 3/4 cup white wine
• 1 tablespoon rose salad vinegar
• 1 tablespoons rose syrup (homemade or from the store).
Serve on small decorative salad plates. Garnish with chopped rose petals with some finely grated lime peel.

Chilled Rose Soup

This is a chilled soup, great for hot summer afternoons. Serve it with tiny cookies for a dessert, or with miniature sandwiches at tea time.

- 4 cups fresh or frozen red raspberries, pureed in a blender
- 2 cups plain yogurt
- 1 cup heavy cream
- 1/2 cup buttermilk
- 2 teaspoons freshly squeezed lemon juice
- 1 cup fresh rose petals
- 1 teaspoon rose syrup
- 2 teaspoons sugar
- Dash of cinnamon

Place the raspberry puree and lemon juice, along with the yogurt in a blender and blend. Add remaining ingredients and blend well. Chill. Serve in small glass bowls that have been well chilled first. Top with fresh rose petals and a mint sprig.

DESSERTS

My friend, Puneet Sharma, originally from New Delhi, India, is an accomplished cook and says that using roses in cooking is as common in India as cinnamon or vanilla is in our country. This recipe is Indian in origin and wonderful for any special occasion.

Puneet's Rose Soufflé

- 2 cups fresh whipping cream
- 2 tablespoons. food grade rose water
- 2 tablespoons. Knox unflavored Gelatin
- 1/3 cup sugar
- 2 tablespoons. water
- 4 egg whites
- Pink or red food color, optional

Puneet's Rose Soufflé, *continued*
For decoration:

- Fresh pink rose petals
- Whipped cream, that's flavored with 2 teaspoons of rose syrup during the whipping process.

Method:

Place a strip of foil around small round soufflé dishes (1/2 cup capacity). Secure with an adhesive tape (collar should be at least 2 inches higher than the dish). Apply melted butter at the base and sides of the dish and inner side of the collar (or spray with cooking spray). Mix sugar and water together and heat until dissolved (do not boil). Remove from heat, stir in rose water, food color and refrigerate for 30 minutes.

- Soak gelatin in water for 1-2 minutes or until dissolved.
- Whisk egg whites in a dry bowl till stiff peaks form using an electric beater.
- Beat cream, slowly adding sugar syrup in medium bowl until whipped.
- Place dissolved gelatin in a chilled bowl and whip until fluffy.
- Add cream mixture and mix gently.
- Fold in whisked egg whites.
- Spoon the mixture into prepared dish until mounded up, full, then refrigerate until set.

Before serving, cut the foil and carefully remove it. Top with dollops of whipped cream that have been flavored with 2 teaspoons of rose syrup. Top with a generous scattering of fresh rose petals.

Candied Rose Petals

This isn't as difficult as it sounds and the petals keep for several months. They are tasty as elegant little after dinner candies, or for use on top of desserts, ice cream, cakes, etc.

Choose fragrant red or pink roses for this. Pick them after the dew has left but before the heat of the day (the fragrance is best then).

You will need:
- 1 egg white, slightly frothed up with a fork
- 1 cup extra fine sugar
- A cookie sheet covered with waxed paper

Pluck the rose petals from the stem. Dip each petal in the egg white, covering both sides, and remove most of the egg white with your thumb and finger. Holding the petal over the waxed paper, sprinkle liberally each petal with the sugar, coating both sides. Lay the petals on the waxed paper. When the cookie sheet is full, or you have run out of roses, put the cookie sheet in the oven.

An oven with a pilot light will dry the petals in about a day, but if your oven has no pilot light that stays on, it will take 4-5 days for your rose petals to dry. You want them to be crisp and dry, enough so that when you try to bend one, it breaks in two. Or, if you have a food dehydrator, dry the petals on the lowest setting.

Store the petals in layers in a jar or any airtight container. Put a layer of petals, topped with a layer of waxed paper or aluminum foil, another layer of petals, etc. Then put the lid on tight. Keep the jar out of light - even fluorescent light in the kitchen will destroy the color. Kept in an air tight container, out of light, the candied rose petals will last several months and can be used as garnish, as after dinner treats or other decorative uses.

Rose Whipped Cream

Rose whipped cream is so utterly delicious as a filling for cakes. I like to make my lemon balm cake in thin layers, spreading rose whipped cream between each layer and scattering fresh blueberries between the layers to hold up the cake (so it doesn't squash out the cream). Then I add a handful of berries on top and add a bit more rose whipped cream and a few rose petals. It's heavenly!

- 2 cups heavy whipping cream
- 3 tablespoons powdered sugar
- 2 teaspoons food grade rose water
- Fresh rose petals for garnish

In chilled bowl, with chilled beater, beat whipping cream until it begins to thicken. Add the rose water and part of the powdered sugar. Continue beating until the cream begins to stiffen. Add remaining sugar and beat until whipped. Chill until ready for serving. Use this on fresh blueberries, raspberries or any other fresh fruit.

Rose Petal Cake

- 1/2 cup plus 2 tablespoons butter
- 2 1/2 cups cake flour
- 1/2 teaspoon salt
- 1 tablespoon baking powder
- 1 1/2 cups sugar
- 3/4 cup milk
- 3 egg whites
- 1/2 teaspoon rum or brandy extract (or 1 tablespoon of rum or brandy)
- 1/2 cup coarsely chopped rose petals
- 1/2 cup sliced almonds
- 1 tablespoon food grade rosewater

Preheat oven to 350 degrees. Mix the wet ingredients together in one bowl. Mix dry ingredients in a separate bowl (not including the rose petals), then combine the wet and dry ingredients together, beating well. Add the rose petals and mix again. It will be somewhat lumpy.

Bake in 2 greased, floured 9" pans for 30 to 35 minutes, or until a toothpick inserted in the center comes out clean. Cool on wire racks.

Frosting for Rose Petal Cake:
- 2 cups whipping cream
- 1 teaspoon vanilla
- 1/3 cup sugar
- petals from 3 fragrant red or pink roses
- candied rose petals, if desired

Whip the whipping cream until soft peaks form. Slowly add sugar and vanilla and continue beating until fully whipped. Spread between layers of cake, stack layers, frost the top and sprinkle rose petals over the top and set on candied rose petals around the top edge of the cake. Refrigerate until ready to serve.

Rose Cake Icing
- 2 cups super fine sugar
- 1/2 stick butter (1/4 cup) at room temperature
- 1/4 cup cream cheese, softened to room temperature
- 2 teaspoon rose syrup (commercial or home made)

Melt butter in microwave until just soft. Stir in the sugar, cream cheese and rose syrup and beat (food processor works great for this). When well blended, spread on cooled white or yellow cake. When frosting has firmed a bit, decorate with candied rose petals or fresh rose petals.

Rose Layer Cake

Bake any favorite yellow cake mix, or make it from scratch, in round cake pans. Let cool and slice the 2 cakes into 4 thinner layers. Spread each layer with Rose Filling (below) and top each layer of the Filling with a layer of fresh, fragrant rose petals. Top the cake with an additional layer  of Filling and sprinkle lavishly with rose petals, adding a whole rose in the center. Don't spread Filling on the sides, you want the layers of rose petals to show. Refrigerate the cake for about an hour before serving, to let the layers set up. (This makes a delightful wedding cake, also)

Rose Filling:
- 1 large package instant vanilla pudding mix
- 3 cups milk
- 1 large (8 oz.) package cream cheese, room temperature
- 3 teaspoons food grade rose water
- 1/2 cup powdered sugar
- 1 small carton Cool Whip

In a food processor, combine all of the ingredients except the whipped topping. Process for about a minute, until everything is well blended. Pour out into a bowl and mix in the whipped topping with a whisk, until there are no lumps. Cover with plastic wrap and refrigerate 30 minutes (or even overnight). Use the Rose Filling for the cake recipe above. This is a delightful, light filling and frosting for cakes, and also works well for the following trifle recipe:

Old-Fashioned Southern Raspberry Rose Trifle

A trifle by English standards is a sponge cake, spread with fruit jam, soaked in wine, broken up and mixed with whipped cream. Here's my version, which is easier, and more suited to American tastes.

Bake any favorite cake recipe, or cake mix. I like the super moist yellow mixes for something fast. Bake the cake and let it cool. To make the trifle, break up the cake into large chunks and place in a bowl, then add the following:

• 2 cups fresh berries (raspberries, strawberries, blueberries, whatever is in season)
• 2 cups fragrant pink or red rose petals
• 4 cups of the Rose Filling recipe from *page 24*

Mix only enough to combine all the ingredients. Chill until ready to serve. Serve in stemmed glasses - a margarita glass is perfect. Top with rose leaf or mint sprig and a few additional berries. Sometimes I top this with 1/4 cup very cold champagne just as the dishes are served.

Rose Sorbet

I use a variety of flowers and fruit juices for sorbets in summer, depending upon what is in season at the time. Lots of kitchen specialty stores, even discount houses, offer inexpensive sorbet makers. My favorite is the kind that you simply hand crank. I can get the inner liner out of the freezer, where I store it, pour in some chilled juice or water with the rose petals and rest of the ingredients, and turn the crank every few minutes while preparing the meal for guests. The sorbet is then ready to serve in chilled glasses as a palate cleanser between courses, or as a light dessert at the end of the meal.

- 1 cup gently packed fragrant red rose petals
- 1 cup superfine or confectioner's sugar
- 3 cups very cold water or sparkling water
- 3 tablespoons fresh lemon juice

Process the rose petals and sugar in a food processor until a fairly smooth paste is formed. Add 1/2 cup of the water and blend for another minute. (I sometimes transfer the paste and water to the blender at this point and blend on high speed for about a minute, to make a smoother texture.) Add the remaining water and lemon juice, pulse blend briefly, then transfer to an ice cream or sorbet mixer and freeze according to manufacturer's directions. (I often chill the sorbet liquid for a few hours, blending briefly once again before pouring into the sorbet freezer. It speeds up the freezing time.) Add a mint sprig and a few rose petals when serving.

Black Tea and Rose Sorbet

This recipe is so good that even the lumber jacks and con-struction workers in your party will rave! I first concocted the recipe for an herb group in Odebolt, Iowa, when I gave a work-shop on "Ten Ways to Eat a Rose, " at Prairie Pedlar Herb Farm's summer festival. The recipe was a big hit and I've made it several times for guests since then.

- 4 cups water
- 1 quart sized tea bag of any good, black China tea
  (or use any regular brand of iced tea bag you normally use)
- 1/2 cup sugar
- Juice of 1 freshly squeezed lemon
- 2 tablespoons rose syrup (homemade or boughten)
- 2 tablespoons chopped, fresh rose petals

Bring water to a boil, add the tea bag and remove from heat. Let steep, covered, for 30 minutes. Remove tea bag and discard. Add sugar, lemon juice and rose syrup, stirring well. Chill for at least 2 hours in the refrigerator. Pour into an ice cream or sorbet freezer and freeze. Serve with rose petals scattered on top.

Tip: Freeze the serving dishes in advance. You can even scoop out the sorbet onto waxed paper in the freezer, then add it to the bowls and let stand at room temperature for 5 minutes before serving.

Rose Syrup Sorbet
Remember to have all of the ingredients well chilled in advance before starting to freeze the sorbet.

- *1 cup rose syrup (from recipe, page 10, or any commercial rose syrup)
- 3 cups water (1 cup set aside for dissolving the sugar)
- Juice of 1/2 freshly squeezed lemon
- 1/2 cup sugar dissolved in 1 cup of the above water

*You can buy ready-made rose syrup at International stores; just substitute 1/2 cup commercial rose syrup and 1/2 cup water.

Combine all ingredients, well chilled, then place in the sorbet mixer and turn on, or hand crank. Sorbet will be ready in about 15 minutes. Serve in chilled champagne glasses with fresh (chilled) raspberries if available. Pour a tablespoonful of chilled rose syrup over the top at serving and garnish with rose petals.

Rose Ice Cream

- 3 cups half and half
- 3 cups heavy cream
- 2 cups milk
- 1 cup sugar
- 2 tablespoons rose syrup
- 1/8 teaspoon salt, optional

Mix thoroughly and pour into electric ice cream mixer and freeze according to mixer's instructions. Serve in frozen dessert glasses with fresh berries and red and pink rose petals.

Cheater's Rose Ice Cream

(It's cheating because you don't actually <u>make</u> rose ice cream, but the flavor is wonderful and it's a simple process).

- 1/2 gallon good quality vanilla ice cream
- 1/4 cup dry fragrant rose petals, ground up (or substitute 3/4 cup finely chopped fresh rose petals)
- 1 tablespoon rose syrup (recipe found elsewhere or use commercial rose syrup)
- 1 tablespoon food grade rosewater
- 1/4 teaspoon ground cardamom

Soften ice cream slightly in a large bowl. Stir in the remaining ingredients until well mixed. Spoon into well chilled (I freeze them for an hour) serving glasses. Top with fresh rose petals.

Rose Creams

These are dainty little cookies, much like meringues. Store in an airtight container.

- 2 cups sugar
- 1/4 cup light corn syrup
- 1/4 cup milk
- 1/4 teaspoon cream of tartar

Combine ingredients and cook over a low heat until sugar dissolves. Raise the heat slightly and continue cooking until the soft ball stage is reached, stirring slowly. Remove from heat and let cool slightly. Add 1/2 teaspoon rose water, color slightly with a drop of red food color and beat mixture until creamy. Drop by teaspoons onto waxed paper and let cool.

Tiny Rose Cookies
Dainty little nibbles for tea time.

- 1/2 cup butter
- 3/4 cup sugar
- 1 egg, beaten
- 3/4 cup flour
- 1/8 teaspoon salt
- 2 teaspoons rose water
- Tiny pinch of mace (less than 1/8 teaspoon)

Mix ingredients and blend thoroughly. Drop spaced apart, like small marbles on a greased cookie sheet. Bake at 370 degrees for 12 minutes, or until lightly browned. Makes approximately 30 little cookies.

Rose Frosting
Use this to ice little tea cakes. Or, use it as an "icing" for fresh blueberry kabobs. For that, use small bamboo skewers and string fresh blueberries on them. Dust with sugar and vanilla powder, then add a bit of rose frosting to the top edges of the blueberries.

- 3 oz. cream cheese, at room temperature
- 1 tablespoon milk
- 2 1/2 cups powdered sugar
- 1 teaspoon food grade rose water (or rose syrup)
- Few drops red food coloring

Combine and mix ingredients. Spread on top of your favorite white cake, cookies, cupcakes, etc., and sprinkle with fresh rose petals for garnish.

Easy Rose Butter
- 1/2 lb. (2 sticks) unsalted butter, room temperature
- 1 1/2 cups fragrant rose petals

Put rose petals in food processor and pulse blend several times until all the petals are chopped. You should have about a cup of chopped petals. Mix the roses with the butter and mix well. Put in pretty bowl and mound up, cover with plastic wrap and refrigerate over night. Remove from refrigerator at least an hour before serving to allow the butter to soften. This is a delicious butter to use on tiny appetizer sandwiches: spread tiny slices of bread with rose butter. Add rose petals like you would lettuce, along with a very thin slice of cucumber. Top with a second slice of bread, also buttered. Cut into decorative shapes if desired. These are beautiful and wonderfully rose flavored!

Sunday Morning Rose Omelet
This is a wonderful "special day" meal, such as for birthdays or anniversaries. Serve it in bed, with a rose in a vase on the side.
- 3 Eggs
- 3 tablespoons water
- 1/4 Teaspoon Rose Water
- 3 tablespoons fresh chives, well chopped (or substitute green onion tops)
- 1/8 cup of your favorite cheese (feta works well, but so does extra sharp cheddar)
- Petals from one large fragrant rose
- Pinch of salt

Cut up the rose petals a bit with scissors and set aside. Separate egg whites and yolks into separate bowls. Add water and rose water and salt to egg whites and whisk until well blended.

Whisk the egg yolks until creamy and fold in the egg whites and chives and whisk again. Pour into medium hot, skillet or omelet pan that's been sprayed with cooking spray; watch for the edges to firm. Using a spatula, fold firm edges into center and tip the skillet so that the still liquid center runs out to form a new edge; continue folding in the firm edges using this process until the omelet is no longer runny, but still wet inside.

Sprinkle cheese and the slivered rose petals on top and place in broiler until cheese is lightly melted. Remove pan from broiler, fold in half, transfer to plate and garnish with additional rose petals and a mint sprig. Serve with fresh fruit, toast and your favorite juice.

Basil Rose Petal Pesto

Use this on pasta dishes or spread on bread with fresh tomato slices, cucumber and lettuce, for an excellent sandwich.

- 2 cups fresh basil (lemon basil is my favorite to use, but use whatever basil is handy)
- 1 cup fragrant rose petals
- 3 cloves garlic
- 1/2 pine nuts
- 1 cup extra virgin olive oil
- 1 teaspoon food grade rose water
- 1 cup Parmesan cheese (freshly grated if possible)
- 1/4 cup Romano cheese (also freshly grated)
- Salt and pepper to taste

Peel and coarsely chop garlic. Combine the basil, garlic and pine nuts in a food processor. Pulse blend a couple of times, then add olive oil and rose water, along with the two cheeses, salt and pepper and pulse blend lightly. Cover and store in refrigerator until ready to use. Can be stored up to 4 days.

BEVERAGES

Rose Petal and Black Tea

Very aromatic, refreshing and soothing on cool winter evenings.

- 4 cups boiling water
- 1 cup fresh, fragrant, pink or red rose petals
- 1 cup size tea bag of any kind of black tea
  (Lipton's, Cain's)

Combine ingredients in teapot, cover and let steep for five minutes. Strain into tea cups and serve.

Rose Geranium and Rose Tea

- 4 cups boiling water
- 2 tea bags of black tea
- 1 rose geranium leaf, fresh or dry
- 1 cup fresh, fragrant rose petals
- 2 whole cloves
- 1 small piece cinnamon stick, about 3/4 inch long

Combine together in teapot and add the boiling water. Cover and let steep for 5-7 minutes and strain into tea cups and serve.

Rose Cooler

A delightful beverage for hot, muggy summer afternoons.

- 1/2 cup rose syrup
- 2 cups cold club soda
- Several fresh rose petals

Combine soda and syrup over ice in a glass, and garnish with rose petals. Makes 2 1/2 cups liquid, or enough for 2 high-ball glasses with ice.

Rose Petal Wine

Loosely fill a 2 gallon glass or plastic container with rose petals. Red petals provide the best color. Add 3 quarts of boiling water and let it steep overnight.

The next day, add the juice and cut up pieces of 2 limes and 4 oranges and stir into the rose petal water. Let that mixture stand for 3 days. Strain through a cheesecloth and discard solids.

Add 2 broken up cakes of yeast (or 2 packages of granulated yeast) and 5 pounds of sugar. Stir well and add enough water to make 2 gallons.

Pour the liquid into sterilized gallon jugs and cover loosely with cheesecloth. Store in moderately cool place until fermentation ceases. This will take at least 4 weeks and possibly as many as ten (fermentation ceases when the liquid quits bubbling). Generally this process takes about 4 to 6 weeks. Strain until clear through cloth. Chill and serve. This is a delicious, sweet wine. From friend, Dotty Peck, who ran the Lake House Bed & Breakfast, Kimberling City, Missouri for many years.

Rose & Spearmint Tea

• 1 cup fragrant rose petals
• 1 fresh sprig of spearmint (about 4 inches long)
• 8 cups boiling water

Pour boiling water over mint and roses, cover container with lid, plate or plastic wrap and let steep for 5 minutes. Pour into mugs and serve hot with 1/2 tablespoon honey per cup. This can also be served over ice.

"Flowers are the friend of physicians and the praise of cooks."
...King Charlemagne

Rose Punch

- 8 rose geranium leaves, dry or fresh
- 2 sprigs (about 4 inches long, about a dozen leaves) fresh lemon verbena
- 1 sprig rosemary
- 4 cups fresh rose petals
- Juice of half a freshly squeezed lemon
- 1 quart fresh or frozen strawberries
- 2 bottles wine (like a rose or sweet white)
- 4 tablespoons mild honey or light brown sugar
- 1 bottle champagne

Bruise the geranium leaves, rosemary, lemon verbena and rose petals with a spoon, adding strawberries and place in bottom of plastic container. Add honey and lemon juice. Pour 1 bottle of wine over the herbs and refrigerate for at least 4 hours (or overnight). Strain, add the second bottle of wine and champaign (both chilled), to the strained liquid, just before serving time. Pour into a chilled punch bowl and serve. Add a rose petal to each glass. Makes approximately 20 four ounce cups. For a nonalcoholic version, substitute 1 bottle of ginger ale and one bottle of sparkling water or tonic water and add a sliced lemon.

Rose Trivia:

The earliest known fossil of a rose ever found, was discovered in Colorado, dating back 40,000,000 years! The oldest known artwork of a rose is found at the Palace of Knossos, in Crete, in the Blue Bird fresco, from the Bronze Age.

The Mediterranean region contributed the Rosa gallica, an important ancestor of our modern cultivated roses. Found in the wild, early roses were single, with 6 petals. But by 300 B.C., Theophrastus described the many forms of roses he grew, including those with one hundred petals. He said that the "hundred-petalled" roses grew on Mount Pangaeus near Philippi, and people were taking cuttings there, for growing around their own homes.

Sources

Food Grade Rosewater:
Heritage Products
Box 444
Virginia Beach, VA 23458
800-862-2923

Rose Syrup:
Asian markets and better quality liquor stores

Old Rose Plants:
The Antique Rose Emporium
www.AntiqueRoseEmporium.com
800-441-0002

High Country Roses
www.HighCountryRoses.com
800-552-2082

The Roseraie
www.Roseraie.com
207-832-6330

Rose Seed:
Jungs Seed (for best fruiting roses)
www.jungseed.com
Fax: 800-692-5864

Renee's Garden Seeds (for miniature, fragrant roses)
reneesgarden.com
831-355-7228
Fax: 831-335-7227

Dried herbs & roses. Books by Jim Long and other Jim Long products:
Long Creek Herbs
P.O. Box 127
Blue Eye, MO 65611
417-779-5450
More recipes on the website: www.Longcreekherbs.com

Index